Dinosaur Reports

PETER SLOAN &
SHERYL SLOAN
Illustrated by Pat Reynolds

About Dinosaurs

The word dinosaur means "terrible lizard." But dinosaurs were not like the lizards that we know today.

There were many kinds of dinosaurs. Some were very large and others were small. The meat-eating dinosaurs were fierce beasts. They had long teeth, powerful legs, and sharp claws.

We know about dinosaurs from the study of their bones, footprints, and eggs. We compare these things to what we know about animals living today.

Tyrannosaurus rex
(king tyrant lizard)

Tyrannosaurus rex was a meat-eating dinosaur.

Tyrannosaurus rex was a big dinosaur. It had a large body and head. Its teeth were long and sharp. It had strong back legs and huge claws.

Tyrannosaurus rex lived in the forests and grasslands.

This fierce dinosaur hunted and killed other animals.

Ankylosaurus
(fused lizard)

Ankylosaurus was a plant-eating dinosaur.

Ankylosaurus was as wide as a tank. It had bony plates on the top of its body. It had spikes on the end of its long, thick tail.

This large dinosaur lived in the grasslands near lakes and rivers.

Ankylosaurus ate plants. It was able to fight well with its heavy tail.

Triceratops
(three-horned face)

Triceratops was a plant-eating dinosaur.

Triceratops had a big body with a large head. On its head it had three horns. Around its neck it had a thick, bony plate.

Triceratops lived in forests and grasslands.

Triceratops cut plants with its tough beak. It ground them up with rows of teeth in the back of its mouth. This dinosaur could run fast.

Brachiosaurus
(arm lizard)

Brachiosaurus was a plant-eating dinosaur.

Brachiosaurus was a huge dinosaur. It was taller than seven people and longer than three buses. It had a big, heavy body with thick legs like tree trunks. This dinosaur had a long neck and a thick tail.

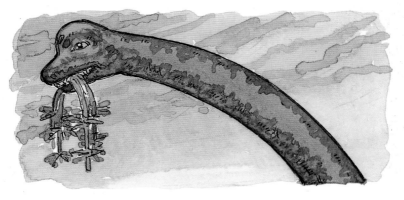

This big dinosaur lived in forests near lakes. It may have spent much of its time standing in the water.

This giant animal used its long neck to reach leaves in the tops of trees. It could crush other dinosaurs with its heavy tail.